California Dreams

Karen Carlson-Kreibohm

Cornelsen

California Dreams

erarbeitet von
Karen Carlson-Kreibohm, Berlin

Verlagsredaktion
Susanne Döpper

Technische Umsetzung
Michael Kolar

Grafik
Gabriele Heinisch, Berlin, S. 4

Bildquellen
James Abram, Berlin, S. 14, S. 15, S. 32 (oben);
Archiv für Kunst und Geschichte, Berlin, S. 26;
Bavaria-Verlag Bildagentur, Gauting, S. 21, S. 28;
Bettmann Archive, New York, S. 36, S. 37, S. 38;
Karen Carlson-Kreibohm, Berlin, S. 18, S. 24;
Cornelsen-Archiv, Berlin, S. 8 (unten rechts), S. 17, S. 25;
Crystal Cathedral Ministries, Garden Grove, CA, S. 39;
Susanne Döpper, Berlin, S. 9 (rechts), S. 11, S. 13, S. 16, S. 31,
S. 32 (Mitte, unten), S. 33;
Angela Herm, Berlin, S. 9 (links);
Bildarchiv Huber, Garmisch-Partenkirchen, S. 8 (oben);
Harald Kertz, Berlin, S. 30 (unten);
Hartmut Tschepe, Berlin, S. 23, S. 30 (oben);
United States Information Service, Bonn, S. 7, S. 12, S. 19, S. 29;
Zentrale Farbbild Agentur GmbH, Düsseldorf, Umschlag

1. Auflage Druck 5 4 3 2 Jahr 98 97 96 95

Alle Drucke dieser Auflage können im Unterricht nebeneinander verwendet werden.

Druck: Adolf Fürst & Sohn, Berlin

ISBN 3-464-05151-X

Bestellnummer 51510

gedruckt auf säurefreiem Papier, umweltschonend hergestellt aus chlorfrei gebleichten Faserstoffen

Contents

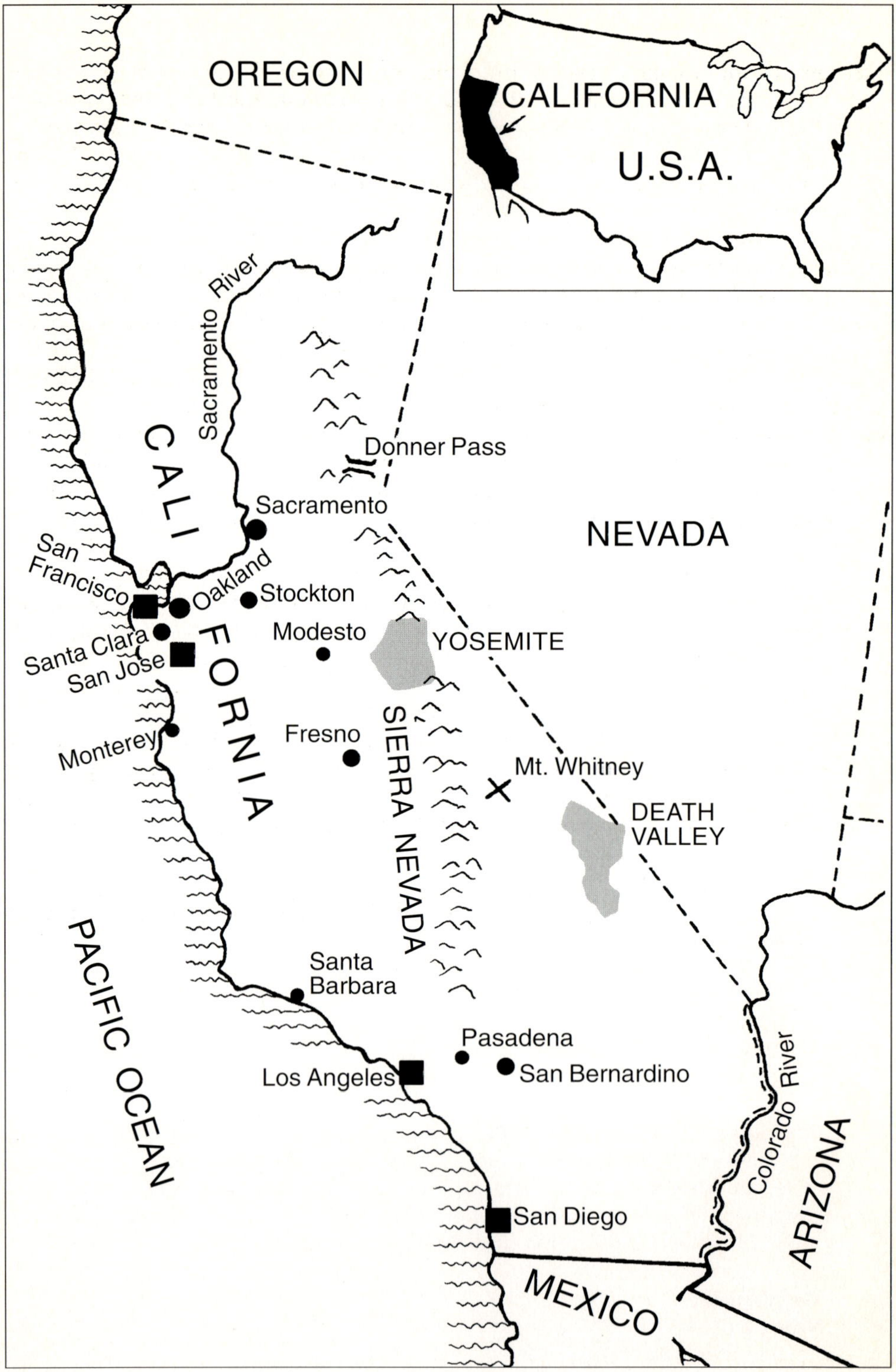
OREGON
CALIFORNIA
U.S.A.
Sacramento River
Donner Pass
Sacramento
NEVADA
CALI
FORNIA
San Francisco
Oakland
Stockton
Modesto
YOSEMITE
Santa Clara
San Jose
Monterey
Fresno
SIERRA NEVADA
Mt. Whitney
DEATH VALLEY
PACIFIC OCEAN
Santa Barbara
Pasadena
Los Angeles
San Bernardino
Colorado River
ARIZONA
San Diego
MEXICO

Dear students,

Whenever people ask me where I'm from and I say "California," the reaction is usually an "Oh" and an "Ah" – almost as if I had said I was from another planet. The next question Germans almost always ask is, "But don't you miss the sunshine here in cold, wet Germany?" Well actually, I don't particularly like hot weather and I don't particularly like to drive either, and those are two unavoidable aspects of life in the Golden State.

But California is still a great place to visit and a great place to have lived for all my school-days, and maybe someday I'll live there again. Yet I know it will never be the same as the place where I grew up. Except for the sunshine and the Pacific Ocean, everything about California is always changing. My family moved from snowy Minnesota to sunny California in 1955 – the same year that Disneyland opened just a few miles down the road from our new house with its four orange trees in the backyard. We walked past orange groves on the way to school and my grandparents lived next to an avocado grove. But the trees are gone now, and the little town called Orange which had a population of 10,000 when we moved there has grown to about 100,000. Every time I return to California, there are more cars, more freeways, more shopping centers, and more people.

When I was in high school, the Beach Boys were at the top of the charts and going to the beach was a favorite pastime for many of my friends. The beaches are still nice, but not everybody in California is a surfer and life isn't one big beach party. Actually, many tourists who expect to spend all day in the sunshine are disappointed because California beaches are usually cool and foggy in the mornings.

People are always saying that California is the world's trend-setter. Whatever happens in America happens first in California. And whatever happens in America later spreads to the rest of the world. If that is really true, California is the place to watch to see how the future of the world might look – probably part dream and part nightmare.

Karen Carlson Kreibohm

PART ONE

"California dreamin'" – What's golden about the Golden State?

The words "California" and "dream" go together like – well – like "Mamas" and "Papas." In the '60s that pop group sang, "I'd be safe and warm, if I was in L.A., California dreamin' on such a winter's day." Dreaming about California means dreaming about warmth and sunshine, beaches and fun.

Since gold was discovered in California in 1848, the California Dream has also meant adventure and risk and the dream of getting rich fast. Hollywood films later added dreams of glamour and fame and a luxurious lifestyle to the image that is all part of the California Dream.

For the thousands of people who keep moving to California every year, the dream is also that of a new beginning and an improvement of their situation as well as a place to try out new ideas. Throughout their history, Americans have kept going west to find new personal freedom and new land, often while at the same time running away from old problems and old traditions. When you reach the Pacific Ocean, you're as far west as you can go. California has also become the goal of thousands of foreign immigrants every year, mostly from Latin America and the Far East. California has taken over the role of New York as the center of new immigrants who each come with their own dreams of America and California.

But besides the California Dream, there's also something which could be called the California Nightmare: a land of smog, earthquakes, crowded freeways, drugs, high prices for land and houses, and lots of rootless, unusual people. The tourist books don't usually mention the fact that California is a place many non-Californians in America love to hate. Some people make fun of Californians and think they spend all their time either working on their suntans, sitting in their cars in freeway traffic jams, or visiting their psychologists. They think it must be somehow unnatural to live in a place without a "normal" climate with cold winters and four seasons.

East Coast intellectuals and Midwest farmers may think that California is a crazy place, but people still keep coming to the state, not just as tourists but to live and work. Since the 1940s, there have been several years when the population of California has grown at the rate of over 1,000 newcomers every day. Today, about 30 million people live in California, 10 percent of all U.S. Americans.

While they all have their own personal dreams and reasons for living in the state, Californians have in common a certain feeling that their state is somehow a special place which is separate and different from anywhere else on earth, almost like an island. Indeed, Spanish explorers, who were the first Europeans who saw what is now California in the 1500s, believed it was an island. They named it after a place described in a popular Spanish novel. In that book, the hero visited an island called California which was "on the right-hand side of the Indies, and very near to the "Earthly Paradise." Only women lived on that island and the only metal found there was gold.

The Golden State

Gold has always fascinated people more than any other metal. Stories about golden cities and about El Dorado, a gold-covered Indian chief, inspired Spanish explorers who came to the New World looking for riches for their home country. But it was an American from New Jersey, James Marshall, who later found gold in California in a river near the present city of Sacramento on January 24, 1848. Marshall wasn't looking for El Dorado, but was working on a sawmill.

Exactly nine days later, the United States signed a treaty with Mexico and made what is now California a territory of the United States. At that time, it took several months for news to travel and no one in the East knew about the gold that had been discovered in the West. But as the news spread, the words "gold" and "California" were suddenly magic words all over the world. Thousands of people, nearly all of them young, unmarried

California gold diggers at the mines

men, began long and difficult journeys to the place which became known as the Golden State. The gold-seekers were called forty-niners because most of them came in 1849. (The name lives on in San Francisco's football team as well as in the song "Clementine" which tells of a "miner, forty-niner" and his daughter.) Few of the forty-niners actually got rich, but just the adventure of finding gold and the idea of owning it was the most exciting thing. Lots of miners had dentists put their gold into their teeth. And if they didn't have any bad teeth, they had the good ones pulled out and gold ones put in. A solid gold smile was their California Dream.

Another kind of gold also became a symbol of California and later attracted even more people to the state than the gold rush. More than any other fruit, sweet golden oranges meant riches and luxury to people who lived in cold climates. Oranges had been the fruit of kings who planted orange trees near their palaces in special gardens called orangeries. While originally an Asian plant, orange trees also grow well in the California sunshine. The citrus boom began in the 1870s when railroads first connected California with the rest of the United States. Every golden orange that arrived in snowy Chicago or Cleveland or Minneapolis advertised the Golden State, a dreamland of luxury and sunshine.

The golden years of Hollywood, especially the 1920s and '30s, when most of the world's films were made there, also spread the idea that California was a land of gold and

Carmel Beach

glitter. Hollywood and the California sunshine also changed people's ideas about beauty and fashion. For hundreds of years, rich people with white skin had used various powders and creams to make their skin look even whiter. A suntanned face was a sign that one was poor and had to work outside in the fields. But largely because of the California sunshine and beaches, the outdoor look was suddenly "in." Having a golden suntan was seen as a symbol of a leisurely, luxurious lifestyle.

An orange tree

The golden poppy, which grows in California, was named the official state flower because it symbolized the gold found in the state as well as the golden sunshine. While freeways and farms and and shopping centers mean fewer and fewer golden poppies in California, there are still many which bloom in the spring and cover the hillsides with gold. In the summertime, when no rain falls in much of California, those hills become very dry and brown. But Californians think positively and don't call it brown, but "golden."

PART TWO

Highest, lowest, biggest, oldest – "firsts" and "mosts" in the land of superlatives

A look at the land

One of the all-time best-selling postcards in California is a picture of orange trees with snow-covered mountains in the background. Oranges and snow are typical contrasts in a state where it's possible to spend the morning surfing at the beach and the afternoon skiing in the mountains. In California you can find every kind of landscape: mountains and deserts, farmland and forests, lakes and ocean beaches.

The highest mountain in the U.S. outside of Alaska is only 70 kilometers from the lowest point in America. Mount Whitney is 4421 meters high and a place named Bad Water in

Death Valley

Death Valley is 86 meters below sea level. In the northwestern part of California, there are some of the wettest places in America, in the southern deserts, some of the hottest and driest places on earth. The highest temperature ever measured in the world – except for once in Libya – was 56.6°C in Death Valley in 1913. The world's record for the deepest snow, 8.4 meters in 1983, was made at Mount Lassen, a volcano in northern California which last erupted in 1917. One record which California doesn't hold is that of largest state: Alaska and Texas are much larger. In square kilometers, California is about as large as all of Germany plus Switzerland.

Sequoia trees in Sequoia National Park

California is also full of botanical superlatives. Among plants which are native to the state are the tallest trees in the world: the coastal redwoods which grow along the northern coast from Monterey to the state of Oregon. The tallest ones are about 110 meters high. The oldest living things on earth are also in California: the bristlecone pine trees. The oldest one is about 4,600 years old. Sequoia trees, a kind of redwood, are only 3,200 years old, but they are the largest living things on earth. Someone has figured out that 40 five-room houses could be built from the wood in the biggest one. Tourists in the last century used stumps of sequoia trees as dance floors. A popular tourist attraction was a "drive-through" tree, a living tree with a "tunnel" cut large enough to drive through. Sequoia trees grow in the Sierra Nevadas, a range of mountains in the eastern part of California which is larger in area than the French, Swiss and Italian Alps combined. The Sierra Nevadas, which are higher than the Rocky Mountains, stretch about 690 kilometers from north to south. Some of California's most beautiful scenery is found in the Sierra Nevadas. The three national parks there are favorite vacation spots.

There is a lower range of mountains along the Pacific coast. Between the mountain ranges is a large, flat valley 720 kilometers long. This land was once covered with sea water. Rotting organic matter from that time has made the central valley now the most fertile farmland in the world. To the north of the central valley there are cone-shaped volcanic mountains. In the south, there are large deserts and farming valleys. Most of the people in California live in towns near the coast from San Francisco to San Diego. However, more and more people are now moving inland to desert areas and the central valley where temperatures are higher, but land is cheaper.

First in agriculture

Although nearly half of California is forests and much of the rest of the land is either desert or endless suburbs of single-family houses and shopping centers, California is still by far the leading agricultural state in the U.S. Everything from almonds and artichokes and avocados to watermelons and walnuts and zucchini grows in California. More than 200 different crops grow in the state and in most of them, California leads the nation in production. The only American crop which isn't grown commercially in California is tobacco. Many towns celebrate their leading crop with parades and festivals every year. There's an Asparagus Festival in Stockton, a Date Festival in Indio, a Begonia Festival in Capitola, and a Garlic Festival in Gilroy with cooking contests. While California may be best-known for its oranges and lemons, actually, the top five agricultural products are milk and cream, cattle, grapes (including those for raisins and wine), cotton, and hay.

It's possible to drive for miles and miles through the great central valley without seeing any people in the fields or any farmhouses such as those in the American Midwest, like on old Lassie TV shows. Many of California's farms are owned by huge corporations, not individual farm families. Some of the large "agribusiness" companies also own and control the processing, packing, shipping, and marketing of the products grown on their land.

California agriculture has always depended on large numbers of seasonal workers. At different times in history, American Indians, immigrants from China and Japan, "Okies" – people from Oklahoma who had lost their own farms in dust storms of the 1930s – and

An oil drill in an orchard near Maricopa

Mexicans have worked in the fields. They often worked for little money and under difficult and unhealthy conditions. Conflicts between landowners and farm workers were dramatically described in John Steinbeck's novels. In the 1960s and '70s, Cesar Chavez, a Mexican-American like most of the farm workers, became the leader of a world-wide grape and lettuce boycott to draw attention to the poor working conditions. In the end farm workers were allowed to form union agreements and receive some benefits. As a reaction to strikes and boycotts and rising labor costs, California agriculture has become more and more mechanized and uses machines instead of people as much as possible. The fields have been called "factories" for growing food.

First in industry and manufacturing

If California were an independent country, it would be the sixth greatest economic power in the world. California not only leads all the other 49 states of the U.S. in agriculture, but it is also number one in industry and manufacturing. Top industries in California are aerospace (airplanes, missiles, and spacecraft), electronics, food processing, clothing, tourism, and entertainment (films and television). All those industries are directly or indirectly related to California's sunny climate.

Clear, mild weather is a great advantage for the aerospace industry. Huge desert areas of southern California are useful for experimenting and testing aircraft. While California had been the scene of some airplane-building since the 1920s, the aircraft industry boom really began in 1940 when the Nazis invaded France and President Roosevelt called for the production of 50,000 military planes a year, at the time an unbelievable number. Most of the military aircraft production took place in California. It meant thousands of new jobs for newcomers to the state. After World War II, the Cold War arms race and the wars in Korea, Vietnam, and the Persian Gulf led to continued growth of the aerospace industry as new aircraft and new weapon systems were developed. The space program also became an important part of the aerospace industry in California where rockets and satellites and space shuttles have all been designed and tested and produced. The great growth of the commercial airline industry has also helped California's aerospace industry and brought money and new jobs to the state. Californians in particular are frequent flyers. The most traveled air route in the world is that between Los Angeles and San Francisco.

Sunnyvale, Silicon Valley

An important part of aerospace technology is electronics, another major industry in California. Some of the first electronics firms in the state started at the beginning of the century as suppliers of radio equipment to ships that came in to San Francisco Bay. Military needs during World War II as well as a growing consumer market after the war caused the electronics industry to boom. Many of the firms are either south of Los Angeles or south of San Francisco near the big engineering departments of Stanford University where students have long been encouraged to relate their research to manufacturing and business needs. The sunny Santa Clara Valley, once famous for its apricots, prunes and walnuts, has so many electronics firms that it is called Silicon Valley. Silicon is the material used for making memory chips. The first integrated circuit, the first microprocessor, and the first personal computer all came out of Silicon Valley.

The most spectacular success story is that of Steve Jobs and his friend Steven Wozniak who invented a personal computer in their garage, the classic place for the biggest and brightest ideas to develop. (California houses seldom have basements, but they always have large garages connected to the houses. The garage often serves as a workshop or hobby room besides a place to keep the car.) Steve Jobs, 21 years old at the time, sold his VW van to get enough money to fill the first orders for the new computers. He named his company Apple because he liked apples and wanted a name that sounded warm and pleasant. McIntosh, by the way, is a kind of red apple grown in the northern U.S. The made-in-a-garage computer became a multi-million dollar business.

Another important industry in California is the clothing business. The needs of goldminers for strong trousers led to the invention of jeans by the German-Jewish immigrant Levi Strauss in the mid-1800s. A new international market for jeans influenced by protest movements and popular youth culture of the 1960s has made the Levi Strauss company one of the largest clothing manufacturers in the world.

Sunny beaches and the magic name Hollywood encouraged the growth of the clothing industry in Southern California. Many of the firms have specialized in colorful, non-traditional sportswear or swim-suits. Others have designed high-style fashions for movie stars. Many of the workers in the clothing industry in Los Angeles are new immigrants from Latin America and Asia who often work cheaply and under controversial conditions.

The most cars

California has more cars, more trucks, more drivers, and more miles of freeways than any other state in the U.S. The influence of the car has been especially great in California which grew up together with the coming of the automobile. As early as 1925, Los Angeles had one car for every three persons, over twice the national average. In those early days, gas was cheap and readily available because of the oil wells in the state. The warm climate made year-round pleasure-driving possible and driving along in one's own car was seen as a part of the Californian Dream of new freedom and new independence. Hollywood stars in luxurious cars and movies with fast cars in exciting chase scenes all helped cars become a status symbol and a part of one's personality.

Cars made it possible for people to live far away from their jobs. Lots of people today drive over two hours each way to get to work. Cars as well as plenty of land also made it possible for the majority of Californians to live in single-family houses. The disadvantage is that everything is spread out so far that in most places, life without a car is practically impossible. There is a large public transportation system in San Francisco, but in most of the state, buses or trains hardly exist and aren't very practical because of the great distances.

The "car culture" led to other typical aspects of modern life: The first supermarket, open 24 hours a day and with a parking lot, and the first department store with customer parking places were opened in California in the 1920s. Because of all the cars, the "drive-in" idea became especially popular in California. People can buy food, mail letters, do their banking, watch a movie, or even attend church without leaving their cars. In the

One of Los Angeles' many freeways

Malibu beach on a foggy morning

1950s, a busy little hamburger drive-in in San Bernadino caught the attention of milk-shake-mixer salesman Ray Kroc who later bought that little place from the McDonald brothers and built an empire on the idea of fast food.

Motels, another typical part of American life, were first built for the new kind of car-driving tourists in California. In the 1920s in San Luis Obispo, a group of tourist cottages with bathrooms, telephones, and garages was called the Milestone Motor Hotel. However, that name didn't fit on a new neon sign, so they shortened Motor Hotel to "Motel" and created a new word at the same time.

Another word blend, and another aspect of the California car culture is smog, a word – and a phenomenon – made of smoke plus fog. Even in Indian times, parts of the Pacific coast were known for their "smog" when smoke from Indians' fires didn't rise, but spread out and was trapped by the mountains and intensified by the sun. Cars are probably responsible for about 60 percent of the smog which is sometimes so bad that school children are not allowed to participate in sports and older people are told to stay indoors. People make jokes about waking up in Los Angeles to the sound of birds coughing, but burning eyes and breathing problems and damage to the states' forests and farm products are really major problems in California. Stricter laws for factories, smog controls on cars, alternative energy sources, and plans for allowing only cars which do not burn gas are ways Californians are trying to control the problem.

PART THREE

Azusa, Alcatraz, and Anaheim – place names as a mirror of California history

Indian names

Today, the word "Malibu" means a 22-mile-long strip of very expensive land along the coast near Los Angeles where lots of movie stars and pop singers like to live. But nobody knows what the old Indian word "Malibu" once meant. In any case, it is one of the place names in California which remind us of the first Californians, the Native Americans.

Before the first Europeans came to what is now California, there were probably about 250,000 Indians living there in a hundred different tribes and dialect groups. These Indians lived a simple, peaceful life. They spent most of their time fishing, hunting or gathering nuts and acorns to eat. Diseases, guns, and alcohol brought into the land by the newcomers were a disaster for the Indians. The palefaces took the Indians' land, cut down plants they needed for food, and felt free to kill them like wild animals or else use them like slaves in mines or fields. Later, many were sent to live on reservations which were on the poorest land that whites didn't want.

The number of Indians dropped to about 17,000 by the early twentieth century. However, because of a high birthrate and migration from other states, the number of Indians in California has now jumped to over 200,000. They are one of the fastest growing minority groups in America. While some are still on reservations and suffer from a number of social problems, especially alcoholism and unemployment, many live in cities and towns and are integrated into American society.

Some place names which come from Indian words are: Azusa, probably meaning skunk, although early settlers said it meant "everything from A-Z in the USA"; Cucamonga, a center of wineries and olive-growing whose name meant sandy place; Tahoe, a brilliant blue, very deep lake on the Nevada border named from an Indian word for lake; Temecula, an old cowboy town meaning "sunlight through the mist", and Yosemite, one of America's most popular national parks, named after a tribe of Indians who were called that by their neighbors – it means grizzly bears.

The famous Half Dome in Yosemite National Park

Spanish names

The first Europeans who explored the California coast were people from Spain who had already started colonies in what is now Mexico. These explorers had with them calendars on which each day was named after a different saint of the Catholic Church. When giving names to places they discovered, they often chose the name of the saint who was celebrated that day. The Santa Barbara Channel, for example, was discovered and named

Santa Barbara Mission

on December 4, 1602, Saint Barbara's Day. (Saint Barbara was a young Roman woman who was beheaded by her father because she had become a Christian.) Later, the place which was settled near there, the present beach resort town, was given the same name, Santa Barbara. In Spanish, "san" and "santa" mean saint. About forty towns in California – from San Andreas and San Bernardino to Santa Monica and Santa Rosa – are named after saints.

Alcatraz

When Spanish explorers discovered a river on August 2, 1769 they gave it the name of the person celebrated that day, "Nuestra Señora de los Ángeles de Porciúncula" (Our Lady of the Angels of Porciúncula). The little town that grew up was called "El Puebla de Nuestra Señora la Reina de los Ángeles" (The Village of Our Lady, the Queen of the Angels) – shortened to Los Angeles. The little village with the longest name grew into the largest city in California. And today its name is usually shortened to just "L.A."

Spanish-speaking people also named many places after a feature of the land or an event which happened there Los Gatos, meaning cats, got its name because of a fight between two wildcats there. Los Cerritos means little hills. Alcatraz is Spanish for pelican. There are still many pelicans on that famous island in the San Francisco Bay which was used as a federal prison from 1934 – 63. Today, the old prison is a tourist attraction.

Although Spanish explorers first sailed along the California coast in the 1500s, it wasn't until 150 years later that Spain became interested in starting settlements there so that England or Russia wouldn't take the land. The Spanish plan for settlements included military forts called "presidios," villages called "pueblos," and missions, which were self-sufficient little villages built around a church. Franciscan "padres" or priests wanted to christianize the Indians and teach them skills such as farming, spinning, weaving, making adobe bricks, and building Spanish-style churches and other buildings. The first mission was begun in 1769 in San Diego. During the next 54 years, twenty others were founded along the California coast. Each one was about a day's journey on horseback from the next.

After Mexico had become independent of Spain in 1822, California was part of Mexico. The land that had belonged to the missions was given to private families, partly so that it could be taxed. The new Mexican government needed money. Other huge areas of land were also made into "ranchos," large cattle ranches. The 1830s and 1840s have often been looked upon as romantic days of "fiestas" – colorful parties with much singing and dancing – and "rodeos" – the time when huge herds of cattle were rounded up and branded. The ranchos were usually named after saints or some feature of the land. Many of these old rancho names are still used today. For example: Rancho Santa Anita (part of it is now a famous racetrack), Rancho San Pedro (the Los Angeles harbor is named after it), and Rancho de Aqua Caliente, meaning hot water because of natural hot springs found there.

A modern Mexican fiesta

Yankees and others

During the rancho days, Yankee traders from the American East Coast began coming by boat around South America to trade clothes and manufactured goods for cattle hides. Many of the hides were taken to Boston where they were made into shoes and other leather goods. So many hides were used for trading in those days that they became known as "California bank notes." Each one was worth about one dollar.

Other Yankees arrived from the east by land. The first ones who reached California were fur trappers led by Jedediah Smith in 1826. Hundreds of miles of desert and wilderness, not enough food and water, no trails, and many Indian attacks made the trip to California impossible for all but the most adventurous. Donner Pass, a mountain pass in the Sierra Nevadas, is named after one such group of newcomers led by George and Jacob Donner of Illinois. In 1846 the group of 87 men, women, and children in 20 wagons spent a horrible winter trapped in the snow in the mountains. Many of them died and those who survived ate the flesh of the dead. The name Death Valley in the desert is also a reminder of the difficulties which settlers had in getting to California. At least one person died there because of the extreme heat.

John August Sutter Memorial

A trading center and meeting point for many of the newcomers to California was Sutter's Fort. Johann August Sutter had left his wife and children and debts in Switzerland in 1834 and went to America to build a colony and fort in the Sacramento Valley. It was on Sutter's land that gold was discovered in 1848. That was the beginning of the greatest western migration as thousands of people from all over the world started out for California. Some of the towns that grew up in the mining areas had names like Whiskytown, Rough and Ready, and Fiddletown (because some of the miners there liked to play the fiddle).

While most of the miners either gambled away their gold or used it to pay the high prices of goods, the people who made the most money from the gold rush were merchants. Four of those merchants, known as the "Big Four," used their money to build the first railroads to California. Stanford University carries the name of Leland Stanford, one of the railroad millionaires who used part of his money to start a university. One of his partners, Collis P. Huntington, gave his name to a popular southern California beach town, Huntington Beach. The town of Barstow was named after the president of the Santa Fe Railroad, William Barstow Strong. One of the directors of the Central Pacific Railroad, however, was so modest that he didn't want his name used for a railway station. So they named the place Modesto. It's now a center of almond-growing and winemaking.

Settlers moving west

As more and more people moved to California at the end of the last century, towns were built up almost overnight. Many of them were named after people who planned them or who had owned the land. Downey, Bakersfield, and Fullerton got their names that way. Other settlers named new towns after their hometowns in the east. There is Ontario (from Canada), Manhattan Beach (from New York), and Norwalk (from Connecticut). People from foreign countries also gave names to their new settlements. A group of Danes called their town Solvang, Danish for sunny meadow. A Polish community gave the name of an actress who lived there, Helen Modjeska, to a canyon in southern California. German settlers who grew grapes at a place on the Santa Ana River named their town Anaheim after the river and the German word for home. Anaheim is better known today as the home of Disneyland. Other German names are Humboldt Bay, named after the scientist and traveler, Alexander von Humboldt, and Mount Goethe, a mountain named after the German writer in 1949 on his 200th birthday.

Beverly Hills and Hollywood were quiet little towns named after places in the east several years before the film industry came to town. But one town in the Los Angeles area got its name from a character in early movies. Tarzana was named after Edgar Rice Burroughs' jungle man, Tarzan. Burroughs, who wrote the Tarzan stories, lived on an estate he called Tarzana in the 1920s. The town that grew up there took the same name.

Selling land and houses to newcomers has long been a big business in California. Many new towns were given names for advertising reasons – names as attractive as possible so that people would buy property there. Some of these names were taken from old legends. Examples: Pomona, from the Roman goddess of fruit; Arcadia, a place in ancient Greece; and Avalon, from the stories of King Arthur. Spanish names and new, made-up names which only looked old and Spanish were used for their romantic appeal. They were supposed to remind people of the old rancho days with a pleasant, leisure lifestyle. Yorba Linda, Mar Vista, La Mirada, and Escondido are some examples. Even El Segundo sounds quite pleasant and romantic. Actually, it means simply the second. It was given to the town by the Standard Oil Company because they built their second oil refinery in California there.

PART FOUR

"Fun, fun, fun"

The California Dream of most tourists who come to the state can be expressed in two words: fun and sun. California's sunny weather and great variety of landscapes have made all kinds of sports and outdoor activities possible. Taking part in sports and selling "fun" have long been favorite pastimes and a big business in the Golden State.

Traditional sports

Horseback riding and horse racing have been popular sports in California since the days of huge Spanish-Mexican ranchos in the early 1800s. Just as horseback riding as a sport developed from the task of riding around a ranch tending the cattle, other activities such as hunting and fishing were once necessary for survival, but are now also done as sports.

Skiing, too, was first simply a way to travel through the mountains in the winter. California's first famous skier, John "Snowshoe" Thompson, was a Norwegian who came to California looking for gold. For 20 years he was the skiing postman of the Sierra Nevadas. On his 90-mile route, he often carried a hundred pounds of mail, food, and household goods to the miners. Especially since the winter Olympics were held in Squaw Valley, California in 1960, skiing as a sport has become more and more popular in the state.

Golf, tennis, and swimming in tanks of water (later called pools) were introduced in California at the end of the last century. At first they were only considered pastimes for rich people. A Los Angeles actor, Wallace Reid, was the first to have a swimming-pool dug into his backyard in the early 1900s. By the 1950s, rising middle-class incomes and new technology made backyard swimming-pools very common in many neighborhoods. Tennis is also available to large numbers of people because there are free public tennis courts in many city parks. Tennis is also offered as a sport in public schools. There are over 700 golf courses in the state. California is famous for many amateur and professional golf tournaments.

California has well-known professional football, baseball, basketball, and ice hockey teams as well as many popular college teams. An important college football game, the Rose Bowl, has been played on New Year's Day in Pasadena since 1916. That annual game has done as much as any other single event to advertise California's mild winter climate to fans who come from cold and icy places in the east to watch the game. Just as famous as the Rose Bowl is the Tournament of Roses Parade, also held in Pasadena on the morning before the football game. What began as a chance for the people of Pasadena to show off their winter roses by decorating their horses and wagons with them in 1889 has now become a huge commercial event. Companies and organizations spend millions of advertising dollars on spectacular, colorful floats. Every inch of all the floats must be covered with flowers or plant material. Hundreds of people bring their sleeping bags and picnic baskets and camp out on the streets of Pasadena for 48 hours before the parade begins so they can have a front-row seat. Millions more watch it on TV every year.

New sports and fun made in California

Besides traditional sports, many Californians also enjoy more unusual or dangerous activities such as skydiving, hang gliding, ballooning, mountain climbing and wild-water racing. Many new sports and activities first became popular in California.

Surfing at Huntington Beach

Surfing is the sport that people associate with California more than any other. Actually, surfing began hundreds of years ago in the Polynesian Islands. The first surfer in California, George Freeth, was brought from Hawaii in 1907 to put on surfing shows and attract people to buy land in the new town of Redondo Beach. Freeth was advertised as the man who could "walk on water." His surfboard was made of solid redwood and weighed 200 pounds. In the early 1950s, a Californian, Bob Simmons, invented a lightweight board of synthetic materials. Surfing soon spread all along the California coast. The Beach Boys' surf-sound hits of the 1960s and a number of popular beach-party films celebrated surfing as a sport as well as a carefree, fun-in-the-sun lifestyle. If you listen carefully to the Beach Boys' "Surfin' U.S.A.", you can hear the names of all the favorite California surfing beaches – from Del Mar and La Jolla near San Diego up to Santa Cruz, south of San Francisco.

Buggy driving near Yuma

Skateboarding or "sidewalk surfing" began when kids first put roller skate wheels on pieces of wood and combined two classic childhood pleasures: scooters and roller skates. The first commercially made skateboards were made and sold in Dana

Scooter = Roller

Point, a California beach town, in 1958. Surfers were among the first who bought skateboards. This way they could practice their skills on days when the waves weren't good for surfing or when they couldn't get to the beach. The first skateboard championships were held in California. Although skateboarding has now become international, nearly all skating equipment (boards, wheels, shoes, clothes, etc.) is made in California.

Frisbees were first called flying saucers in 1957, a time when Hollywood film makers and the American public were particularly fascinated by the idea of UFOs. The Wham-O Company of San Gabriel, California made those first flying saucers which became popular toys along the wide, sandy California beaches. When the president of Wham-O went on a tour of east coast college campuses to advertise his flying saucers, he discovered that students at Yale University in Connecticut were already playing a similar game with metal pie pans they called "frisbies." They were called that because each one was marked with the name "Frisbie" from the Frisbie Pie Company of Bridgeport, Connecticut, a bakery whose products were popular among the college students. Wham-O renamed their plastic flying saucers "Frisbees," changing the spelling of the original pie company. And they've been flying around the world ever since.

Hula hoops were introduced to the world at about the same time as frisbees by the same people at Wham-O in San Gabriel. Bamboo rings had been used like hula hoops in Australian sports classes, and hoops had been around for hundreds of years as toys in various parts of the world. But it was Wham-O that started making them out of plastic in 1958 and started an advertising campaign that made hula hoops an international fad.

Video arcade games are another California first. The world's first coin-operated video game was invented in 1969 by the research engineer Nolan K. Bushnell in Santa Clara, a town in the middle of California's Silicon Valley , the region famous for all its electronics and computer companies. Bushnell named his new game company "Atari." That's a Japanese expression from the game of Go and it means "prepare to be attacked." Atari's first successful product, a ping-pong-like video game called "Pong," was first played in Sunnyvale, California. In video game history, it is considered the great-grandfather of all arcade video games. Most of the Pong games which were sold, however, were Japanese-made imitations of Bushnell's original game.

Disneyland, etc.

The secret of Disneyland's success is that everything there is better than the real thing. When designing monkeys for Disney's jungle, for example, they found that synthetic fur was of much better quality than real monkey fur to use for animals that climb trees electronically. Disneyland has a jungle without tsetse flies, New Orleans without humidity, pirate ships without scurvy, bobsled rides down the Matterhorn without ice and snow, and a small town without crime or litter or parking problems.

Disneyland was created by Walt Disney, the father of Mickey Mouse and Donald Duck, and opened on July 17, 1955 in the middle of orange groves in Anaheim, California. Later, similar parks were built in Florida, Japan, and Europe. The idea behind Disneyland is a typical California Dream: taking technology and imagination and money and creating a new artificial reality where everybody who comes is a part of the show. In a way, all of California is based on that Disneyland idea.

Mickey Mouse, Disneyland

Children love the place, of course, but it's designed for grown-ups, too. Disneyland plays with emotions and memories of mythical good old days. The streets and shops and horse-drawn wagons of "Main Street" are all built a bit smaller than in real life, creating a cosy, friendly feeling. Particularly in Southern California, where more people than in any other state have moved in from somewhere else, Disneyland creates the feeling of a hometown, a memory of a place and time that never existed, but people wish it had. Disneyland is also super-clean – armies of young Disney workers dressed in white attack every gum wrapper or piece of popcorn as soon as it falls to the ground. Lots of Californians have season tickets and come to Disneyland several times a month just to walk around and shop and feel at home.

Of course Disneyland is more than nostalgia. It also takes visitors into the future. One of the most popular rides is "Star Tours," designed by the California-born film maker George Lucas (*Star Wars*). The ride creates the perfect illusion of traveling wildly through space although you don't even leave your seat. The seats wiggle and jerk as you sit in the dark and watch a movie screen and hear "space sounds" coming from all directions.

Not far from Disneyland is one of its biggest rivals, Knott's Berry Farm. The Knott family used to have a boysenberry farm there in the 1920s. They sold their berries as well as Mrs. Knott's jams and berry pies from a little roadside stand. To earn some more money during the difficult depression days, they started serving chicken dinners to travelers. To attract more customers and to entertain them while they waited for their dinners, the Knotts began to bring in old buildings that had been used in cowboy movies. Knott's Berry Farm grew and grew into a huge Wild West town complete with stagecoach rides and an old-fashioned train that gets robbed several times a day. While not exactly typical of the Wild West days, Snoopy and Charlie Brown and their friends walk around the park, too. Their pictures are used on Knott's Berry Farm's advertising and T-shirts and souvenirs much like Mickey Mouse and Donald Duck and Pluto are used as symbols of Disneyland. Charlie Brown's creator, Charles Schulz, also lives in California.

A stagecoach ride at Knott's Berry Farm

California has lots of other attractions designed for entertaining tourists. One popular place is Sea World in San Diego, where whales, dolphins and penguins do their tricks for the tourists. San Diego is also the home of one of the world's largest and most famous zoos. For those who like roller coasters and exciting fast rides, Magic Mountain near Los Angeles is the place to go.

The famous killer whale show at Sea World, San Diego

Forest Lawn, where death is a pleasure

Only in California could a cemetery be made into a tourist attraction and funerals and death be mixed with show business. Forest Lawn Memorial Park is a cemetery in the hills above Los Angeles, where soft music plays from loudspeakers hidden in the rose bushes. Many famous Hollywood stars and California personalities are buried here in parts of the park which have names like "Slumberland" and "Whispering Pines." Tourists come to drive their cars through the gardens and admire the reproductions of all of Michelangelo's major sculptures. There's also a huge stained-glass version of Leonardo da Vinci's painting *The Last Supper* presented as a show with light and sound effects. Exact copies of famous old English and Scottish country churches built within the cemetery are just as popular for weddings as they are for funerals. In 1917, the founder of Forest Lawn, a banker named Dr. Hubert Eaton, said he wanted to create a place as "unlike other cemeteries as sunshine is unlike darkness."

PART FIVE

"It never rains in Southern California"

Water and weather

California has plenty of water. The problem is that it's in the wrong places. Most of it is in the rivers and lakes and melting snow of the north, but 80 percent of the people and farms are in the south. Another problem is storing the water when rainstorms come to the south. "It never rains in Southern California ..." is only the first line of the song. It goes on, "... but girl, don't they warn ya, it pours, man, it pours." It doesn't rain at all in southern California from May to October, and not very often in the winter or spring, either. But when the rains come, it pours violently and non-stop for several days at a time. Streets become canals, and expensive houses built high on hills with fantastic ocean views slide down the hillside. There's an old saying: When it rains in New York, people get wet; when it rains in California, people get killed.

Southern Californians enjoy their warm, dry climate and the idea of planning a summer picnic or beach party or sports event without even thinking about the possibility of rain. They also enjoy swimming-pools and golf courses and green grass and clean cars and daily showers – and don't think about the fact that their land is really a huge dry desert. Farmland in the state is the richest in the world, but only when it gets enough water. And rain water alone is never enough. California farms depend completely on the technology of irrigation systems.

Fighting about water rights has been a problem as long as California has been a state. Some of the most violent fights were at the beginning of the century when Los Angeles began to grow into a big city, but had hardly any water. A great aqueduct was built to carry water 400 kilometers from a mountain river to the city. Farmers along the way who lost much of their own water because of the project dynamited it several times. A dam which was part of the system broke in 1928. It flooded a town and killed 400 people.

Today, the state has a huge system of aqueducts, canals, dams, reservoirs, pumping stations, and power stations to move water hundreds of miles throughout the state from mountains in the north and the Colorado River in the east to the central and southern farming

Irrigating crops

valleys and coastal cities. There have been suggestions for building a pipeline to bring water from Alaska down to California – a distance of over 2,250 kilometers. Another idea is to bring in huge blocks of ice from Antarctica. Most water plans are not only very expensive, but also very controversial because of the resulting changes and damages to the natural environment.

Fires

Besides water problems, another consequence of California's dry climate is the danger of fires. Several houses burn down every few years when there is a major forest fire. Most of those houses are built with a lot of wood and are on hillsides. Hot, dry desert winds can carry tiny sparks and cause fires to spread over huge areas and burn thousands of acres. Even if the fire is miles away, owners of houses with wooden roofs sometimes get on their roofs with garden hoses. They get the roofs wet so that if a flying spark lands there, it won't start to burn so easily.

While fires today are usually caused by a careless cigarette-smoker or a campfire not put out properly, actually, forest fires and "brush fires" – brush is the name for short dry bushes which cover many California hills – have been part of California's ecology for thousands of years. The natural plant and animal life is adapted to having fires every few years and even depends on them. The seeds of some kinds of plants, for example, need to have extremely high temperatures before they can start to grow. But of course today, in a place where millions of people live, fires are only seen as a major problem and danger.

Earthquakes

An aspect of California geography which has influenced the land since prehistoric times is the fact that California sits on top of one of the world's major earthquake belts. The

Fire in Sacramento Street after the great earthquake of 1906

largest and best-known fault, an area where two huge plates of land come together, is the 1,100-kilometer-long San Andreas fault. It begins in the Pacific near the Oregon border and goes through San Francisco, the San Joaquin Valley and into Southern California to Mexico. One land plate moves slowly southeast, the other northwest. As these plates pull against each other, the earth's crust is stretched like a giant rubber band and sometimes it snaps – causing an earthquake. There are hundreds of other smaller faults in California. Actually, there are earthquakes every day in the state, but nearly all of them are so small that people can't feel them.

But big ones are disasters. The most famous earthquake happened on April 18, 1906 in San Francisco. It began at 5:13 in the morning when the ground shook for two minutes. Although some buildings were destroyed by the earthquake, the greatest damage was caused by the fires which began when gas lines broke and chimneys fell down and broken water pipes made it difficult to fight the flames. In three days, the fire destroyed about one-third of the buildings in San Francisco and caused 500 deaths.

San Franciscans always refer to the disaster as "the fire" – not the earthquake. That's a typical attitude in California: People always hear warnings about the "Big One," a major earthquake that will hit the state some day, but they avoid thinking about it. It's usually tourists and newcomers to the state who worry more about earthquakes. Others make jokes about buying land in Nevada so they'll have some beach-front property after California falls into the sea.

There are quite strict rules in California so that houses and bridges and buildings, particularly schools, are as earthquake-safe as possible. Scientists are always trying to find out how to tell when an earthquake may be coming – by studying the earth, watching the behavior of animals, and even looking to the moon and stars for clues. There are earthquake drills where everybody is told to go to a safe place (under a table or against an inside wall) and stay there for 30 seconds until they hear the all-clear signal on the radio. And after every large earthquake, like the one in the Santa Cruz area in October 1989 which killed 67 people and caused six billion dollars worth of damage, there's always a big business selling extra bottled water and canned food and flashlights and blankets to people who want to be prepared for the next one. But the most common attitude is that there's nothing we can do about it anyway, so let's go to the beach and enjoy life. This is California.

PART SIX

Cities and symbols – the Golden Gate Bridge and the Hollywood sign

London has its Big Ben, Paris its Eiffel Tower, and Berlin the Brandenburg Gate. California's two best-known cities, San Francisco and Los Angeles, also have world-famous symbols which make a statement about the feeling and history and style of those places.

The Golden Gate Bridge

Probably no other bridge in the world is photographed as often as the Golden Gate Bridge in San Francisco. Although the bridge is painted a golden-red color, the narrow entrance to San Francisco Bay was actually named the Golden Gate long before the bridge was built and even before gold was discovered in California. A mapmaker called it the Golden Gate because he believed the harbor would someday be a gateway to the golden treasures of the Orient. It still plays that role today, but those treasures from Asia are now video recorders and televisions, cars and jogging shoes.

Although people had had the idea of building a bridge across the bay since the beginning of the century, construction wasn't begun until 1936 as part of a public works program to give jobs to people during the depression. Changing tides, violent storms, and the need to make the towers earthquake-safe made the bridge construction especially difficult. For many years, it was the longest suspension bridge in the world. There are 1,280 meters between the two 227-meter-high towers, the world's highest. There is enough steel wire in the cables to go around the world three and a half times. It takes about twenty minutes to walk across the bridge – a favorite tourist activity. It's also a popular place to jog – as well as a "favorite" place to commit suicide.

The Hollywood sign

The Hollywood sign

The Hollywood sign has also been used as a jumping off place for suicide. In 1932, jumping down the hill from the top of the letter "H" was the way a depressed, unemployed actress chose to die. Each of the white metal letters in the sign is as high as a five-story building.

The sign has been in the hills above Hollywood, which is part of Los Angeles since 1923. Originally, the sign was put up to advertise a new housing development. At that time, the recently arrived film industry was changing the town from a quiet, church-going community of lemon-growers into a noisy, glamorous center of newly rich stars and film producers. In those early days of Hollywood, a man named Albert Kothe lived in a little hut beside one of the "L"s. His job was to change light bulbs: there were 4,000 of them on the sign, placed every 20 centimeters.

As radio and television began to take away the glow from Hollywood's golden days, the sign suffered, too. The wind blew down some of the letters and the lights were all either stolen or shot out. But plans to take down the sign have always been met with great protests and save-the-sign campaigns. Enough private individuals and businesses – many from the entertainment world – are found who are willing to give thousands of dollars necessary to save the famous symbol. Major repairs were made in 1984 in time for the summer Olympics in Los Angeles.

San Francisco

A favorite hobby of San Franciscans is complaining about how awful everything is in Los Angeles and how glad they are that the don't live there. They see L.A. as nothing but smog and freeways and chaos with no real beginning and no real end. San Francisco, on the other hand, is often called "everyone's favorite city" because of its beautiful setting and its special atmosphere. The city is built on the hills on a relatively small peninsula

San Francisco skyline

Lombard Street

Chinatown

with the Pacific Ocean or the Bay on three of its sides. People and houses and businesses are all closer together than in many American cities and there's a stronger feeling of neighborhood and tradition. San Francisco is often called the most European of all American cities because of its size and cosmopolitan feeling as well as its traditional interest in art and music and literature. Jack London and Mark Twain are among the many writers who have lived in the city. Typical for the San Francisco spirit is a freeway that ends in the air: San Franciscans protested that the new freeway would disturb their skyline and also bring too many new people into the city, so construction was stopped in the middle.

San Francisco's international atmosphere goes back to gold rush days when the town boomed as the arrival point for gold-hungry miners from around the world. The first quicklybuilt tent settlements on the sand soon were replaced by wooden saloons and hotels and theaters, many of which were often destroyed by fires and then built up again.One of the largest groups of foreigners who came to the city were Chinese people. They worked in the gold mines and later on the new railroad lines which connected the continent from east to west. They were excellent workers and willing to work for low wages, which often led to conflicts with white workers. Today, San Francisco's Chinatown is the largest Chinese settlement outside of Asia. San Franciscans and tourists enjoy visiting its shops and restaurants. Films and books have also been based on dramatic scenes in Chinatown's crime world, underground tunnels and opium dens.

A cable car in front of some typical wooden Victorian San Francisco houses

Second only to the Golden Gate Bridge, San Francisco's other most popular attraction is also related to transportation: the cable cars. These old wooden cars run on tracks and travel up and down the city's hills by connecting to an endless, moving cable under the street. They have been part of the city's atmosphere as well as an important means of transportation since 1873. A plan to stop using them was met with such strong protests that they are now protected as historical landmarks (the only landmark on wheels). Both natives and tourists enjoy an exciting ride and like to get out and help turn the cars around at the end of the line.

Cable cars were invented because the streets of San Francisco are so steep that horses had difficulty pulling wagons up the hills. As in most American towns, streets were planned on paper like a checkerboard. In San Francisco, that meant that streets were built perfectly straight and didn't follow the natural curves of the hills. A part of one of the streets is so steep (40 degrees) that to drive on it, cars have to zig-zag down the hill in a series of sharp S-turns. Lombard Street is known as the crookedest street in the world.

Hollywood and Los Angeles

When a large mail-order store in Germany tries to get the attention of its customers by offering a prize of two weeks in Hollywood, it is doing what advertising people always do: using words as symbols and playing with images and atmosphere. They can't mean Hollywood the "real" place, a district of Los Angeles which isn't even on the beach, as the pictures in the advertisement suggest. Hollywood is a relatively normal town with grocery stores and churches and old people's homes. Today, most Hollywood neighborhoods don't have homes of world-famous stars, but of new immigrants from all over the world. At Hollywood High School, over 60 different languages and dialects are spoken. Hollywood also has souvenir shops, restaurants, big record stores, and plenty of "characters" on the street. Tourists like to look at the footprints and handprints of stars in the cement courtyard of Mann's Chinese Theater, an old movie theater built in the style of a Chinese pagoda and the scene of many film premieres. And you can visit your favorite stars at the Hollywood Wax Museum. But that's about all that's directly in Hollywood.

Humphrey Bogart's hand- and footprints in front of Mann's Chinese Theater

A mural near Hollywood Boulevard, Hollywood

The Hollywood Bowl, a popular open-air stage

The "Wild West" stunt at Universial Studios, Universal City.
The studios, which are still used, can be visited by tourists.

Downtown Los Angeles

Of course, writers from that advertising company, as well as most people who use the word, don't mean Hollywood the place, but Hollywood the idea. They mean sunshine and stars and peeking behind the curtains of the rich and famous – even though most of them don't live in Hollywood, but in Beverly Hills or Bel Air. And the movie studios aren't in Hollywood any more either, but in Burbank and other parts of L.A. In fact, no major film was ever made directly in Hollywood. But that doesn't matter. It also doesn't matter that holly doesn't grow in Hollywood either, and never has. In 1886 a woman who had moved from Kansas to a big country house in the middle of a fig orchard near Los Angeles named her new estate Hollywood after a place in Illinois because she liked the sound of the word. But then the first movie-makers came west, too. They liked the sunny area as a practical place to make films. And they liked being close to the Mexican border. At that time, there were bitter conflicts about patent rights for filming techniques and it was helpful to get as far away from New York lawyers as possible.

Hollywood is only one small part of Los Angeles, California's largest city both in population and area. But just as Hollywood is often used to mean the entertainment business and all the luxurious aspects of California life rather than the actual geographical place on a map, Los Angeles is also often used as a general term for much of Southern California – often the negative aspects like smog and crowded freeways and social problems. What is sometimes called the "L.A. area" is a huge mass of houses, stores, offices, factories and endless straight, wide streets all connected by the world's largest freeway system. At rush hour, it is often called the world's largest parking lot. Unless you happen to notice a sign, you can't tell where one city ends and another one begins. Los Angeles is the first large city in the world which grew up in the automobile age. From the beginning, it has spread out in all directions and nothing is within walking distance of anything else.

There is a place called "Downtown" with a city hall, some skyscraper office buildings, and a cultural center for concerts and plays, but it's not a normal downtown with department stores (they've all moved out to the big shopping centers) and tourists (most tourists who fly in to L.A. International Airport don't visit the downtown area at all). But there are plenty of banks and financial offices, as Los Angeles has taken over San Francisco's traditional role of banking and financial center of the West Coast. Many businesses from Japan and other Asian countries also have their main offices in Los Angeles and own property in the city. In fact, the Japanese own about a third of Los Angeles' downtown office space – which leads to jokes about L.A. being Japan's fastest growing city.

Geographically, there is both a Los Angeles County – population about eight million – and within it, a city called Los Angeles with a population of over three million, the second largest in the U.S. The actual city of Los Angeles has rather crazy borders including a zig-zagging strip which connects it to Los Angeles Harbor, the busiest in the country in dollar value. There are also some "islands" of independent cities within the L.A. city limits – Beverly Hills is the most famous one.

Since the 1980s, whites – that is, people whose ancestors came from Europe – have become a minority in L.A. The city is such a mixture of different racial and national groups, that no one group has a majority. L.A. is said to have more Mexicans than Mexico City, more Koreans than Seoul and more Filipinos than anywhere outside any city in the Philippines. About a fourth of the population is Spanish-speaking people from Mexico as well as other Latin American countries. Many of them live in slum neighborhoods of East Los Angeles where street gangs, violence and drugs are part of daily life. Latin Americans – also called Hispanics or Latinos – and Asian-Americans are the fastest growing minorities. While gang-fights and ancient prejudices within the various groups create many social problems, there are also plenty of success stories of immigrants who have managed to get their own California Dream of a good education and a good job – often a business of their own. In many California schools and colleges, Asian-Americans finish at the top of their class. While about one-sixth of the L.A. population is black, the number is slowly going down as new Asian or Hispanic immigrants are moving into black neighborhoods. Some blacks feel bitter about all the new immigrants and think the newcomers are being treated better than they were. Many blacks are moving out to other suburbs and in some cases, back to states in the South where they hope to find better chances for jobs and safer neighborhoods for their children.

Sacramento and other cities

Los Angeles and San Francisco are the best-known cities in California, but neither one is the capital. Sacramento, at about 550,000 only the seventh largest city in the state, is the center of California's government. It was chosen because when California became a state in 1850 gold had just been discovered near Sacramento and the growing town was an important trading center. Sacramento uses its history as a tourist attraction. Sutter's Fort, where the gold rush started, is now an outdoor museum. Once a slum area, Old Sacramento has been made into a tourist center of shops and restaurants with wooden sidewalks and horse-drawn wagons and cobblestone streets like in the days of the Old West. The city's most popular museum is the California State Railroad Museum where visitors can experience the sights and sounds of the golden days of railroading when Sacramento was the western terminus of the new coast-to-coast railroad line. (In most of America today, trains are so rare that people only experience them in museums or places like Disneyland.)

California has about 40 cities with populations of over 100,000. San Diego, a port city near the Mexican border and home of a large Navy base, has over a million people and is number two in population after Los Angeles. It was once considered a rather sleepy place with quiet retired people and wealthy tourists who stayed at places like the Hotel del Coronado and enjoyed the pleasant climate and ocean views. That luxurious old hotel became famous as the scene of Marilyn Monroe's film "Some Like It Hot." San Diego is now one of the most popular, fast-growing cities in the state and a center of aerospace and electronics as well as oceanographic research and fishing. California's largest zoo is in San Diego and the city is also the home of several colleges and universities.

The third largest city in California (San Francisco is only fourth) is San Jose with about 750,000 people. In the 1980s it was considered the fastest growing city in the world. While it had been (and still is) a packing and shipping center for fruits and vegetables, San Jose has also become a center of the electronics industry of Silicon Valley. It's a typical California city without a real center and without much personality, but with shopping centers and miles and miles of straight streets and single-family houses. As author Gertrude Stein once said about Oakland, another California town (and it could be said about most California towns), "there's no there there."

PART SEVEN

"California girls"

Charlotte Parkhurst and others – "firsts" for California women

It was only after her death in 1879 that people found out that Charley Parkhurst (born 1812), one of the toughest stagecoach drivers of the Santa Cruz Mountains, was really a woman – Charlotte Parkhurst. Charley, who was called "Cock-eyed Charley" because she was blind in one eye (a horse had once kicked her in the face), was an expert driver for the Wells Fargo Express Company in the 1860s. In those days, stagecoach drivers were heroes whose dangerous job meant fighting against bad roads, storms, and outlaws to deliver everything from mail to mail-order brides.

Sally Ride

Charley was also active in local politics and often gave speeches for political candidates. She was the first woman voter in California. Women didn't legally get the right to vote until 1911, but since everyone thought Charlotte was Charley, she began voting in the election of 1868.

Later, California women didn't have to dress up like men to follow adventurous careers. Sally Ride, America's first woman astronaut, is from California. So was Georgia Broadwick, the first woman who parachuted from an airplane (in 1913 over Griffith Park in Los Angeles). Other women in the air were the first airline stewardesses. In the early days of flying, it was Ellen Church's idea that passengers would feel safer if there were trained nurses on board. Church, a nurse, suggested the idea to United Airlines in 1930 and became the first stewardess on a flight from Oakland, California to Wyoming. There were eleven passengers on board.

Sarah Winchester and others – spirits, cults and psycho-groups

The Winchester rifle is called "the gun that won the West" because it was used in so many fights with Indians in the western part of the U.S. Sarah Winchester (1840–1922), wife of the inventor of those famous guns, inherited a huge amount of money that had been made by the rifles. But Sarah had a problem: she was afraid that the spirits of all those killed by Winchester rifles would come back and haunt her. A woman who claimed she

Sarah Winchester's Mystery House

communicated with the spirit world told Sarah that the spirits would be confused if she always kept building on her house. She would stay alive as long as she kept building. So Sarah had carpenters work on her house 24 hours a day for 38 years. The result is known today as the Winchester Mystery House, a crazy 160-room tourist attraction near San Jose. The house has 10,000 windows, 2,000 doors, stairs which lead to nowhere, doors that open onto empty walls, and lots of secret passageways. Winchester was fascinated by the number thirteen: there are rooms with thirteen windows, thirteen lights are in the chandeliers, there are stairs with thirteen steps.

Sarah Winchester was one of many Californians who have been attracted to spiritualism (belief in communicating with the spirits of the dead), the occult (supernatural, magical things), as well as all kinds of unusual ideas about psychology. Some people say it's California's warm climate that encourages so many new ideas and experiments and eccentric people. In the 1930s *Life* magazine called the Los Angeles area "this lovely place, cuckoo land" because of all the eccentrics. Most Californians have left behind them old roots and traditions. Many are willing to try anything and believe anybody who promises them a way to find gold at the end of the rainbow. Or at least some new way of dealing with their personal problems.

Throughout California history, many groups of believers in some new idea have lived together in colonies such as the one founded in 1900 at Point Loma, near San Diego, by Katherine Tingley. Believers wore Greek costumes while growing chickens, vegetables and silkworms and practicing a kind of yoga. They founded a Yoga college, opera house and Greek theater and published several books. At the time, more traditional Californians were afraid that the group was bad advertising for the state. Newspapers were filled with "shocking" stories about their strange practices and their holy dog, Spot, who was supposed to be the reincarnation of one of Mrs. Tingley's many dead husbands. The Ojai Valley near Santa Barbara (not far from Nancy and Ronald Reagan's ranch) has long been a center for esoteric groups – those who believe they can discover secret or hidden knowledge. One of the leaders of an esoteric group, Annie Besant, decided that Ojai was the magnetic center of the earth.

Another place in California which is known for its new ideas and experiments with new lifestyles is the Esalen Institute on the coast near Big Sur. The goal of this organization is to combine Western psychology with Eastern philosophy. Some top names in philosophy, psychology and physics, as well as hundreds of other people, many from the business and entertainment world, have all spent time there looking for Truth through new kinds of experiences with their minds and bodies.

Non-Californians have always enjoyed laughing about all the psycho-groups in California and the accent on touch-me-feel-me. They tell the joke: How many Californians does it take to change a light bulb? Answer: Ten – one to change the bulb and nine to share the experience.

While most of the unusual groups are generally tolerated and accepted as part of the colorful California landscape, sometimes the joke isn't funny at all. The most dramatic cult tragedy was in 1978 when Jim Jones and his "People's Temple" of San Francisco moved to South America and all 900 of them committed suicide together.

Aimee Semper McPherson – religion in the land of show business

"Sister Aimee" arrived in Los Angeles in 1922 with two children, an old car, a hundred dollars, and the wish to start a new church and share her ideas about Christ with the people of California. Three years later Aimee Semper McPherson (1890–1944) had collected over a million dollars from her followers and had built Angelus Temple – a church with 5,000 seats, a brass band, huge women's choir, and collection of costumes more colorful and astonishing than that of any theater. McPherson, an attractive blond, wore those costumes at her fantastic religious shows where she would jump around on stage with a pitchfork in her hand to drive out the devil. Sister Aimee was very popular with her fans – mostly lower-middle-class, lonely, dissatisfied people. When she once returned to Los Angeles after having strangely disappeared for several days, she was welcomed by airplanes which covered her arriving train with flowers, and bands, horses and 100,000 cheering people on the street.

Aimee Semper McPherson

Crystal Cathedral, Garden Grove

While California is famous for its many unusual "churches," such as Sister Aimee's, there are also more traditional religious groups. In fact, because Californians have come from everywhere, nearly every religious group in the world is represented in California – as well as lots of new groups first organized in the Golden State. But even among the moretraditional groups, California style, including Hollywood and Disneyland, has influenced religious life. Many churches have large, colorful neon signs and worship services which often include an element of show business. For example: soloists who sing while a symphony orchestra on cassette plays along with them. The California climate as well as a sense of drama led to the tradition of outdoor church services in parks and on mountains at sunrise on Easter morning. The most popular one is held at the famous Hollywood Bowl outdoor theater.

Probably the best-known church in California is the so-called "drive-in" church in Garden Grove where people can choose either to sit in their cars on the church parking lot and listen to the service on their car radio or else go inside a huge glass building called the Crystal Cathedral. This church enjoys drama and special effects, too. Its Christmas shows include flying angels and live camels and sheep. At Easter, there's a simulated earthquake.

Barbie Roberts – forever young, forever beautiful

When Ruth Handler noticed how much her little daughter Barbie enjoyed playing with paper dolls that looked like beautiful young women, she suggested to her toy-maker husband, one of the founders of Mattel Toy Company, that little girls might enjoy playing with a doll that looked like a woman, not a baby or child. The result: "Barbie," who became the most successful doll in toy history. (The company decided her last name was "Roberts" because many young fans wanted to know.)

Barbie was "born" in 1959 in Hawthorne, California, a Los Angeles suburb which is the home of Mattel Toys. It's also the hometown of the Beach Boys who created their California surf-sound only two years later and began singing about California girls, "the cutest girls in the world." Blond and beautiful Barbie was a real California girl – complete with swim-suits and her own swimming-pool, sportswear for all kinds of sports, a horse, waterbed, sports car, ten-speed bike, and enough clothes for a lifestyle full of parties and shopping trips.

But while concerned parents have criticized Barbie for representing a world full of luxury and materialism and think that Barbie dolls encourage little girls to think too much about beauty and boyfriends, Barbie has also given girls new roles to identify with, other than that of mother to a baby doll. Barbie has had the clothes and equipment to be an astronaut, doctor and pilot as well as the old favorites – bride and princess. While Barbie may be seen as a sex symbol, she is also an independent woman. After all, she has her own sports car, and boyfriend Ken – named after the Handlers' son – just comes along for a ride when she invites him.

While the original design for Barbie's face and figure was based on a drawing in the German *Bildzeitung*, Barbie is still a typical California girl. The dream of a perfect figure, perfect face, perfect tan, and perfect hair have led to huge businesses in California where aerobics and jazz dance and body building have become more popular than anywhere else. And not just for teenagers and people under thirty. When she was over fifty, California actress Jane Fonda was still making millions of dollars on her exercise videos which tried to convince women that they could have a Barbie-doll figure at any age.

If fitness centers and exercise videos aren't enough, there's always plastic surgery. Southern California is a center of cosmetic surgery and magazines there are filled with advertisements of doctors who will fix your nose or breasts or hips or whatever isn't perfect. And many of the customers aren't older women looking for a facelift, but teenagers who can afford to buy a new nose as easily as a new dress.

Hollywood films have greatly influenced our ideas about beautiful women – and men, too. Max Factor, a Polish immigrant who had been a wig-maker and make-up man for the Russian ballet, created a kind of make-up for Hollywood stars which would stand up under the camera lights. Before Hollywood, make-up had been seen as something just for prostitutes. But businesses like Max Factor made make-up available and acceptable to millions of American women.

Also important for the right California look is of course the "perfect tan" – skin which the sun has turned golden-brown, but not red and burnt. This became possible after the invention of suntan lotion, which was developed to protect U.S. soldiers fighting in the Pacific during World War II. That military need made it possible for the Beach Boys to sing 20 years later about Califonia girls: "the west coast has the sunshine and the girls all get so tan."

Whether they're looking for a perfect tan, a perfect body, a new religious or psychological experience, an adventure on the edge of the continent, or just a good job and good money, California is the place where the girls – and the boys and the men and the women – keep coming. Everybody keeps looking for their own personal California Dream.

Vocabulary

AE = American English, *BE* = British English, *adv.* = adverb, *n.* = noun, *sb.* = somebody, *sth.* = something

A

acceptable [ək'septəbl] annehmbar, zulässig
acorn ['eɪkɔ:n] Eichel
acre ['eɪkə] Morgen
adapted [ə'dæptɪd] angepaßt
adobe brick [ə'dəʊbɪ brɪk] (ungebrannter) Lehmziegel
(to) **admire** [əd'maɪə] bewundern
adventurous [əd'ventʃərəs] abenteuerlich
(to) **advertise** ['ædvətaɪz] werben
advertisement [*AE:* ædvər'taɪzmənt; *BE:* əd'vɜ:tɪsmənt] Anzeige
advertising *(n.)* ['ædvɜ:taɪsɪŋ] Werbe-
aerobics [eə'rəʊbɪks] Aerobik
aerospace ['eərəʊspeɪs] Flugzeug- und Raumfahrt-
after all schließlich
agreement [ə'gri:mənt] Abkommen
agribusiness ['ægrɪbɪznəs] Agrar(groß)geschäft
agricultural [ægrɪ'kʌltʃrəl] landwirtschaftlich
agriculture [ægrɪ'kʌltʃə] Landwirtschaft
aircraft ['eəkrɑ:ft] Luftfahrzeug
airline ['--] Fluggesellschaft
almond ['ɑ:mənd] Mandel
amateur [*AE:* 'æmətʃʊr; *BE:* 'æmətə] *hier:* Amateur-
angel ['eɪndʒl] Engel
annual ['ænjʊəl] jährlich
appeal [ə'pi:l] Reiz
apricot ['eɪprɪkɒt] Aprikose
aqueduct ['ækwɪdʌkt] Aquädukt
arcade [ɑ:'keɪd] Passage, Spielhalle
arms Waffen
artichoke ['ɑ:tɪtʃəʊk] Artischoke
asparagus [ə'spærəgəs] Spargel
(to) **associate** [ə'səʊʃɪeɪt] in Verbindung bringen
avocado [ævə'kɑ:dəʊ] Avokado

B

background ['--] Hintergrund
backyard ['-'-] *AE: Garten hinter dem Haus*
bakery ['beɪkərɪ] Bäckerei
ballet [bæ'leɪ] Ballett
ballooning [bə'lu:nɪŋ] Ballonfahren
bamboo [bæm'bu:] Bambus
banker Bankier
banking Bankwesen
basement ['beɪsment] Keller
begonia [bɪ'gəʊnɪə] Begonie
(to) **behead** [bɪ'hed] enthaupten
belt [belt] Gürtel
berry ['berɪ] Beere
billion ['bɪlɪən] *AE:* Milliarde
birthrate ['bɜ:θreɪt] Geburtenrate
blend [blend] Mischung
(to) **bloom** [blu:m] blühen
blond [blɒnd] blond; Blondine
bobsled ['bɒbsled] Bob
(to) **boom** [bu:m] boomen
botanical [bə'tænɪkl] botanisch
bottled ['bɒtld] abgefüllt
boycott ['bɔɪkɒt] Boykott
boysenberry ['bɔɪznberɪ] Boysenbeere *(Kreuzung aus Brombeeren, Himbeeren und Loganbeeren)*
(to) **brand** [brænd] mit einem Brandzeichen kennzeichnen
brass band ['bræs 'bænd] Blaskapelle
breast [brest] Brust
bristlecone pine ['brɪslkəʊn 'paɪn] *Kiefernart*
bride [braɪd] Braut
buggy ['bʌgɪ] *AE: leichter Wagen,* Buggy

C

cable ['keɪbl] Kabel
campus ['kæmpəs] Universitätsgelände

canned ['kænd] eingemacht
canyon ['kænjən] Canyon
carefree ['--] sorglos, heiter
cattle ['kætl] Rindvieh
cement [sɪ'ment] Zement
championship ['tʃæmpɪənʃɪp] Meisterschaft
chandelier [ʃændə'lɪə] Kronleuchter
chaos ['keɪɒs] Chaos, Durcheinander
charts [tʃɑ:ts] Hitliste
chase [tʃeɪs] Jagd-
checkerboard ['tʃekəbɔ:d] Schachbrett
childhood ['tʃaɪldhʊd] *hier:* Kindheits-
chip ['tʃɪp] Chip
(to) **christianize** ['krɪstʃənaɪz] christianisieren
citrus ['sɪtrəs] Zitrus
city hall ['--'-] Rathaus
clothing ['kləʊðɪŋ] Bekleidung
clue [klu:] Hinweis, Spur
cobblestone ['kɒblstəʊn] Kopfsteinpflaster
cock-eyed [kɒk'aɪd] schielend
collection [kə'lekʃn] Sammlung
cone-shaped ['kəʊnʃeɪpt] kegelförmig
contest ['kɒntest] Wettbewerb
controversial [kɒntrə'vɜ:ʃl] kontrovers, umstritten
cosmetic surgery [kɒz'metɪk 'sɜ:dʒərɪ] Schönheitschirurgie
cosmopolitan [kɒzmə'pɒlɪtn] international, weltstädtisch
costume ['kɒstju:m] Kostüm
courtyard ['kɔ:tjɑ:d] Hof
crooked ['krʊkɪd] krumm
crop [krɒp] Feldfrucht
crust [krʌst] Kruste
cuckoo ['kʊku:] verrückt
cult [kʌlt] Kult
curve [kɜ:v] Kurve
cute [kju:t] niedlich, hübsch

D

date Dattel
debt [det] Schuld
depression [dɪ'preʃn] (Welt-) Wirtschaftskrise
disease [dɪ'zi:z] Krankheit
(to) **disturb** [dɪ'stɜ:b] stören
doll [dɒl] Puppe
dolphin ['dɒlfɪn] Delphin
drill [drɪl] Drill, Probe
(to) **dynamite** ['daɪnəmaɪt] sprengen

E

earthly irdisch
eccentric [ɪk'sentrɪk] exzentrisch
ecology [i:'kɒlədʒɪ] Ökologie
electronics [ɪlek'trɒnɪks] Elektronik
emotion [ɪ'məʊʃn] Gefühl
empire ['empaɪə] Reich, Imperium
(to) **erupt** [ɪ'rʌpt] ausbrechen
esoteric [esəʊ'terɪk] esoterisch
estate [ɪ'steɪt] Landsitz

F

facelift ['--] Facelift(ing), Gesichtshautstraffung
fad [fæd] Masche, Mode
fame [feɪm] Ruhm
fault [fɔ:lt] *hier:* Verwerfung
feature ['fi:tʃə] Merkmal
fiddle ['fɪdl] Fiedel, Geige
fiesta [fɪ'estə] Fest
fig orchard ['fɪg ɔ:tʃəd] Feigenplantage
(to) **figure out** [--'-] ausrechnen
(to) **fix** [fɪks] reparieren, in Ordnung bringen
flesh [fleʃ] Fleisch
float [fləʊt] Festwagen
footprint ['--] Fußabdruck
forever [fər'evə] immer
fort [fɔ:t] Fort
Franciscan [fræn'sɪskən] Franziskaner-
freeway ['--] Autobahn
frequent ['fri:kwənt] häufig
front-row ['frʌnt'rəʊ] in der ersten Reihe
funeral ['fju:nrəl] Beerdigung
fur [fɜ:] Pelz, Fell
fur trapper ['træpə] Pelztierjäger/in

G

(to) **gamble** ['gæmbl] (um Geld) spielen, wetten
garlic ['gɑ:lɪk] Knoblauch
gateway ['geɪtweɪ] Tor
(to) **gather** ['gæðə] sammeln
geographical, geographically [dʒi:ə'græfɪkl/ɪ] geographisch
glamour ['glæmə] Glanz
glamourous ['glæmərəs] glamourös, glanzvoll
glitter ['glɪtə] Glitzern
glow [gləʊ] Schein, Leuchten
goddess ['gɒdəs] Göttin
golf course ['gɒlf kɔ:s] Golfplatz
goods Waren, Güter
grape [greɪp] Weintraube
grizzly bear ['grɪzlɪ] Grislybär
grove [grəʊv] Plantage
growth [grəʊθ] Wachstum

H

handprint ['--] Handabdruck
(to) **haunt** [hɔ:nt] spuken, verfolgen
hay [heɪ] Heu
hang gliding ['hæŋ glaɪdɪŋ] Drachenfliegen
happen: unless you happen to notice wenn du nicht zufällig bemerkst
hide [haɪd] Haut, Fell
hip [hɪp] Hüfte
Hispanic [hɪ'spænɪk] Hispano-Amerikaner/in; hispanisch; spanischsprechend
holly ['hɒlɪ] Stechpalme
hometown ['-'-] Heimatort
horrible ['hɒrɪbl] schrecklich
horseback: on horseback ['--] zu Pferd
horse-drawn ['--] von Pferden gezogen
hose [həʊs] Schlauch
housing development ['haʊzɪŋ dɪ'veləpmənt] Wohnsiedlung
hula hoop ['hu:lə hu:p] Hula-Hoop-Reifen
humidity [hju:'mɪdətɪ] Luftfeuchtigkeit

I

illusion [ɪ'lu:ʒn] Illusion
imitation [ɪmɪ'teɪʃn] Nachahmung
income ['--] Einkommen
(to) **inherit** [ɪn'herɪt] erben
inland ['--] landeinwärts
integrated ['ɪntɪgreɪtɪd] integriert, eingegliedert
integrated circuit ['sɜ:kɪt] integrierter Schaltkreis
intensified [ɪn'tensɪfaɪd] verstärkt
(to) **irrigate** ['ɪrɪgeɪt] bewässern
irrigation [ɪrɪ'geɪʃn] Bewässerung

J

(to) **jerk** [dʒɜ:k] ruckeln
jungle ['dʒʌngl] Dschungel

K

(to) **kick** [kɪk] treten
Korean [kə'rɪən] Koreaner/in; koreanisch

L

labor *(AE)* **= labour** *(BE)* ['leɪbə] hier: Arbeits-
landmark ['--] Wahrzeichen
(the) **Last Supper** ['sʌpə] (das) Letzte Abendmahl
Latino [læ'ti:nəʊ] Lateinamerikaner/in
lawn [lɔ:n] Rasen
lettuce ['letɪs] Kopfsalat
lifestyle ['--] Lebensstil
litter ['lɪtə] Abfall
lotion ['ləʊʃn] Lotion

luxurious [lʌg'ʒʊərɪəs] luxuriös
luxury ['lʌkʃərɪ] Luxus

M

made-up ['-'-] erfunden
magnetic [mæg'netɪk] magnetisch
(to) **manage** ['mænɪdʒ] es fertigbringen
marked [mɑ:kt] gezeichnet
mass [mæs] Masse
manufactured goods [mænjʊ'fæktʃərd] industriell hergestellte Waren
manufacturer [mænjʊ'fæktʃərə] Hersteller/in
manufacturing [mænjʊ'fæktʃərɪŋ] Herstellung
marketing ['---] Marketing, Verkauf
materialism [mə'tɪərɪəlɪsm] Materialismus
matter ['mætə] Stoffe
meadow ['medəʊ] Wiese
mechanized ['mekənaɪzd] mechanisiert
merchant ['mɜ:tʃənt] Kaufmann/frau
microprocessor ['maɪkrəʊprəʊsesə] Mikroprozessor
migration [maɪ'greɪʃn] Abwanderung
mild [maɪld] mild
millionaire ['mɪljəneə] Millionär/in
missile [*AE:* 'mɪsl; *BE:* 'mɪsaɪl] Rakete
mission ['mɪʃn] Missionsstation
mist [mɪst] Nebel, Dunst
mixture ['mɪkstʃə] Mischung
modest ['mɒdɪst] bescheiden
movement ['mu:vmənt] Bewegung
mural ['mjʊərl] Wandgemälde
mystery ['mɪstərɪ] *hier:* Rätsel-, Geheimnis-
mythical ['mɪθɪkl] mythisch

N

Navy base ['neɪvɪ 'beɪs] Marinestützpunkt
neon ['ni:ɒn] Neon
newcomer ['---] Neuankömmling
nightmare ['naɪtmeə] Alptraum
Norwegian [nɔ:'wi:dʒən] Norweger/in
nostalgia [nɒ'stældʒə] Nostalgie
nut [nʌt] Nuß

O

(the) **occult** [*AE:* ə'kʌlt; *BE:* 'ɒkʌlt] (das) Okkulte, Übersinnliche
oceanographic [*AE:* əʊʃnə'græfɪk; *BE:* əʊʃənəʊ'græfɪk] meereskundlich
olive ['ɒlɪv] Olive
Olympics [ə'lɪmpɪks] Olympische Spiele
opera ['ɒprə] Oper
opium den ['əʊpɪəm den] Opiumhöhle
orangery ['ɒrɪndʒrɪ] Orangerie
organic [ɔ:'gænɪk] organisch
Orient ['ɔ:rɪənt] Orient, Morgenland
outlaw ['--] Bandit/in

P

pagoda [pə'gəʊdə] Pagode
paleface ['peɪlfeɪs] Bleichgesicht
(to) **parachute** ['pærəʃu:t] mit dem Fallschirm abspringen
paradise ['pærədaɪs] Paradies
(to) **participate** [pɑ:'tɪsɪpeɪt] teilnehmen
partly zum Teil
pass [pɑ:s] Paß
passageway ['pæsɪdʒweɪ] Gang
pastime [pɑ:staɪm] Zeitvertreib
patent ['pætnt] Patent
(to) **peek** [pi:k] verstohlen gucken
pelican ['pelɪkən] Pelikan
peninsula [*AE:* pə'nɪnsələ; *BE:* pə'nɪnsjʊlə] Halbinsel
phenomenon [fə'nɒmɪnən] Phänomen
philosophy [fɪ'lɒsəfɪ] Philosophie
pie [paɪ] *runder Obstkuchen aus Mürbeteig*
pie pan ['paɪ pæn] rundes Kuchenblech
pilot ['paɪlət] Pilot/in
ping-pong ['pɪŋpɒŋ] Tischtennis
pipe [paɪp] Rohr
pipeline ['paɪplaɪn] Rohrleitung
pirate ['paɪrət] *hier:* Piraten-
pitchfork ['pɪtʃfɒk] Heugabel
planet ['plænɪt] Planet

plate Platte
pool [puːl] Schwimmbecken
popcorn [ˈpɒpkɔːn] Popcorn
poppy [ˈpɒpɪ] Mohnblume
(to) **pour** [pɔː] gießen
powder [ˈpaʊdə] Pulver
premiere [*AE:* prɪˈmɪər; *BE:* ˈpremɪeə] Uraufführung
presidio *(Spanish)* [prɪˈsɪdɪəʊ] Fort
priest [priːst] Priester/in
processing [ˈprəʊsesɪŋ] Verarbeitung
professional [prəˈfeʃnəl] beruflich
property [ˈprɒpətɪ] Besitztum, Grundstück
prostitute [ˈprɒstɪtjuːt] Prostituierte
prune [pruːn] Backpflaume
psycho-group [ˈsaɪkəʊgruːp] *Gruppe, die einer bestimmten psychologischen Richtung anhängt*
psychologist [saɪˈkɒlədʒɪst] Psychologe, Psychologin
psychology [saɪˈkɒlədʒɪ] Psychologie
pueblo *(Spanish)* [ˈpwebləʊ] Dorf
purple [ˈpɜːpl] lila

R

railroad [ˈreɪlrəʊd] Eisenbahn
rainbow [ˈreɪnbəʊ] Regenbogen
raisin [ˈreɪzn] Rosine
ranch [*AE:* ræntʃ; *BE:* rɑːntʃ] Ranch, Viehfarm
range [reɪndʒ] Gebirgskette
rate [reɪt] Tempo
rather than [rɑːðə] eher als
redwood [ˈ--] Redwood
refinery [rɪˈfaɪnərɪ] Raffinerie
reincarnation [riːɪnkɑːˈneɪʃn] Reinkarnation, Wiedergeburt
relatively *(adv.)* [ˈrelətɪvlɪ] relativ
reminder [rɪˈmaɪndə] Erinnerung
(to) **rename** [riːˈneɪm] neu benennen
reproduction [riːprəˈdʌkʃn] Reproduktion
research [ˈriːsɜːtʃ] Forschung
reservoir [ˈrezəvwɑː] Reservoir
residency [ˈrezɪdntsɪ] (herrschaftliches) Wohnhaus
retired [rɪˈtaɪəd] pensioniert
ride [raɪd] Fahrt
rocket [ˈrɒkɪt] Rakete
rodeo [ˈrəʊdɪəʊ] Rodeo
roller coaster [ˈrəʊlə kəʊstə] Achterbahn
roller skate [ˈrəʊlə skeɪt] Rollschuh
romantic [rəʊˈmæntɪk] romantisch
rootless [ˈruːtlɪs] wurzellos
rotting [ˈrɒtɪŋ] verfaulend
(to) **round up** [ˈ-ˈ-] zusammentreiben
rush [rʌʃ] Rausch
rush hour [ˈ--] Hauptverkehrszeit

S

said: L.A. is said to have von L.A. heißt es, daß es ... hat/L.A. soll ... haben
saint [seɪnt] Heilige/r
saloon [səˈluːn] Saloon
sawmill [ˈsɔːmɪl] Sägewerk
scooter [ˈskuːtə] Roller
scurvy [ˈskɜːvɪ] Skorbut *(Vitamin-C-Mangelkrankheit)*
seasonal [ˈsiːzənl] Saison-
self-sufficient [selfsəˈfɪʃnt] selbstversorgend
sequoia [sɪˈkwɔɪə] Mammutbaum, Sequoie
setting [ˈ--] Lage, Umgebung
shipping [ˈ--] Versand
(to) **show off sb./sth.** [ˈ-ˈ-] vorführen, angeben mit
shuttle [ˈʃʌtl] Raumtransporter
sidewalk *(AE)* [ˈ--] Bürgersteig
silkworm [ˈsɪlkwɜːm] Seidenraupe
simulated [ˈsɪmjʊleɪtɪd] simuliert, vorgetäuscht
(to) **ski** [skiː] Ski laufen
skunk [skʌŋk] Stinktier
skydiving [ˈ---] Fallschirmspringen
skyline [ˈ--] (Stadt-)Silhouette, Skyline
(to) **slide** [slaɪd] rutschen
slum [slʌm] Slum
Slumberland [ˈslʌmbəlænd] Schlummerland
smog [smɒg] Smog
solid [ˈsɒlɪd] massiv
soloist [ˈsəʊləʊɪst] Solist/in

someday ['--] eines Tages
souvenir [su:və'nɪə] Souvenir, Andenken
(to) **snap** [snæp] zerbrechen
spacecraft ['speɪskrɑ:ft] Raumfahrzeug
spark [spɑ:k] Funke
spectacular [spek'tækjʊlə] spektakulär, sensationell
spinning ['spɪnɪŋ] Spinnen
spirit ['spɪrɪt] Geist
spiritualism ['spɪrɪtʃʊelɪzm] Spiritismus
sportswear ['--] Freizeitkleidung
spot [spɒt] Ort, Stelle
spring Quelle
stagecoach ['steɪdʒkəʊtʃ] Postkutsche
stained-glass ['steɪnd'glɑ:s] Buntglas-
stand (Verkaufs-)Stand
status ['stætəs] Status
steep [sti:p] steil
stewardess [*AE:* 'stu:ərdəs; *BE:* 'stju:ə'des] Stewardeß
storing ['stɔ:rɪŋ] Lagern, Aufbewahren
(to) **stretch** [stretʃ] strecken
strip [strɪp] Streifen
stump [stʌmp] Stumpf
stunt [stʌnt] Schaunummer
sunrise ['--] Sonnenaufgang
suntan ['sʌntæn] Sonnenbräune
superlative [su:'pɜ:lətɪv] Superlativ
supernatural [su:pə'nætʃrəl] übernatürlich
surgery ['sɜ:dʒərɪ] Chirurgie
suspension bridge [sə'spenʃn] Hängebrücke
(to) **symbolize** ['sɪmbəlaɪz] symbolisieren
symphony orchestra ['sɪmfənɪ 'ɔ:kɪstrə] Sinfonieorchester
synthetic [sɪn'θetɪk] künstlich, synthetisch

T

tan [tæn] braun; Bräune
tank [tæŋk] Tank
temple ['templ] Tempel
(to) **tend** [tend] hüten
term [tɜ:m] Bezeichnung
territory ['terɪtɔ:rɪ] Territorium
terminus ['tɜ:mɪnəs] Endstation
tide [taɪd] Ebbe und Flut, Tide
tolerated ['tɒləreɪtɪd] toleriert, geduldet
tough [tʌf] rauh, hart
tournament ['tɔ:nəmənt] Turnier
trader ['treɪdə] Händler/in
trail ['treɪl] Pfad
transportation system *(AE)* [trænspɔ:'teɪʃn] Verkehrssystem
trapped [træpt] wie in einer Falle gefangen
treasure ['treʒə] Schatz
treaty ['tri:tɪ] Vertrag
trend-setter ['trend setə] jd./etwas, der/das richtungsweisend ist
tsetse fly ['tsetsɪ] Tsetsefliege

U

UFO [ju:ef'əʊ] = **unidentified flying object** UFO, unbekanntes Flugobjekt
unavoidable [ʌnə'vɔɪdəbl] unvermeidbar
union ['ju:nɪən] Gewerkschaft

V

version ['vɜ:ʃn] Version
Victorian [vɪk'tɔ:rɪən] viktorianisch
volcano/s [vɒl'keɪnəʊ/z] Vulkan/e

W

walnut ['wɔ:lnʌt] Walnuß
warmth [wɔ:mθ] Wärme
watermelon ['wɔ:təmelən] Wassermelone
wax [wæks] Wachs
wealthy ['welθɪ] wohlhabend
weaving ['wi:vɪŋ] Weben
whale [weɪl] Wal
whatever [-'--] was auch immer
Whispering Pines ['wɪspərɪŋ 'paɪnz] Flüsternde Kiefern
wig [wɪg] Perücke
wiggle ['wɪgl] wackeln

wilderness ['wɪldənɪs] Wildnis
winery ['waɪnərɪ] Weinkellerei
wrapper ['ræpə] Papier, Verpackung

Y

ya [jæ] you
Yankee ['jæŋkɪ] Amerikaner/in *(Spitzname)*
yoga ['jəʊgə] Yoga

Z

(to) **zig-zag** ['zɪgzæg] Zickzack laufen
zucchini [zʊ'ki:nɪ] Zucchini

Names

Family names

Barstow ['bɑ:stəʊ]
Besant [bə'sænt]
Bogart ['bəʊgɑ:t]
Broadwick ['brɔ:dwɪk]
Burroughs [*AE:* 'bɜ:rəʊz; *BE:* 'bʌrəʊz]
Bushnell [bʌʃ'nel]
Chavez [ʃə'ves]
Disney ['dɪsnɪ]
Eaton [i:tn]
Factor ['fæktə]
Fonda ['fɒndə]
Freeth [fri:θ]
Handler ['hændlə]
Huntington ['hʌntɪŋtn]
Jobs [jɒbs]
Knott [nɒt]
Kothe ['kəʊθɪ]
Kroc [krɒk]
Lucas ['lu:kəs]
McPherson [mk'fɪərsn]
Parkhurst ['pɑ:khɜ:st]
Reagan ['reɪgn]
Reid [ri:d]
Roosevelt ['rəʊzəvelt]
Schulz [ʃʌlts]
Semper ['sempə]
Simmons ['sɪmənz]
Stanford ['stænfɔ:d]
Stein [staɪn]
Steinbeck ['staɪnbek]
Strauss [straʊs]
Thompson ['tɒmpsn]
Tingley ['tɪŋglɪ]
Twain [tweɪn]
Winchester ['wɪntʃestə]
Wozniak ['wɒznɪæk]

Girls/women

Aimee ['eɪmɪ]
Annie ['ænɪ]
Barbie ['bɑ:bɪ]
Charlotte ['ʃɑ:lət]
Georgia ['dʒɔ:dʒə]
Gertrude ['gɜ:tru:d]
Katherine ['kæθərɪn]
Nancy ['nænsɪ]
Ruth [ru:θ]

Boys/men

Albert ['ælbət]
Cesar ['seɪzɑ:]
Collis ['kɒlɪs]
Edgar ['edgə]
Hubert ['hju:bət]
Humphrey ['hʌmfrɪ]
Jacob ['dʒeɪkəb]
Jedediah [dʒedɪ'daɪə]
Ken [ken]
Leland ['li:lənd]
Levi ['li:vaɪ]
Max [mæks]
Nolan ['nəʊln]
Ray [reɪ]
Ronald ['rɒnəld]
Wallace ['wɒlɪs]
Walt [wɔ:lt]

Place names

Alcatraz ['ælkətræz]
Anaheim ['ænəhaɪm]
Arcadia [ɑ:'keɪdɪə]
Avalon ['ævəlɒn]
Azusa [ə'zu:zə]
Bakersfield ['beɪkəzfi:ld]
Bel Air ['bel 'eə]
Beverly Hills ['bevəlɪ 'hɪlz]
Big Sur [sɜ:]
Bridgeport ['brɪdʒpɔ:t]
Capitola [kæpɪ'təʊlə]
Connecticut [kə'netɪkət]
Cucamonga [ku:kə'mʌŋgə]

Dana Point ['deɪnə 'pɔɪnt]
Del Mar ['del 'mɑː]
Donner Pass ['dɒnə]
Downey ['daʊnɪ]
El Segundo [el sə'gʌndəʊ]
Escondido [eskən'diːdəʊ]
Fresno ['freznəʊ]
Fullerton ['fʊlətn]
Gilroy ['gɪlrɔɪ]
Hawthorne ['hɔːθɔːn]
Hollywood Boulevard ['bʊləvɑːd]
Humboldt ['hʌmbəʊlt]
Huntington Beach ['hʌntɪŋtn 'biːtʃ]
Illinois [ɪlə'nɔɪ]
Indio ['ɪndɪəʊ]
Korea [kə'rɪə]
La Jolla [lə 'hɔɪə]
La Mirada [lʌ mɪ'rɑːdə]
L.A. ['el 'eɪ] = Los Angeles [*AE:* lɒs 'ændʒələs; *BE:* lɒs 'ændʒəliːz]
Los Cerritos [lɒ se'riːtəs]
Los Gatos [*AE:* lɒs 'gɑːtəʊs; *BE:* lɒs 'gætəʊs]
Malibu ['mælɪbuː]
Mar Vista [mɑː 'vɪstə]
Maricopa [mærɪ'kəʊpə]
Minneapolis [mɪnɪ'æpəlɪs]
Modesto [mɒ'destəʊ]
Modjeska [mə'dʒeskə]
Monterey [mɒntə'reɪ]
Mount Lassen [maʊnt 'læsn]
Mount Whitney ['wɪtnɪ]
Nevada [ne'vɑːdə]
New Jersey [*AE:* nuː 'dʒɜːzɪ; *BE:* njuː '--]
Norwalk ['nɔːwɔːk]
Oakland ['əʊklənd]
Ojai ['əʊhaɪ]
Oklahoma [əʊklə'həʊmə]
Ontario [ɒn'teərɪəʊ]
Oregon ['ɒrɪgn]
Pasadena [pæsə'diːnə]
Persian Gulf ['pɜːʒən 'gʌlf]
Philippines ['fɪləpiːnz]
Point Loma ['ləʊmə]
Polynesian Islands [pɒlə'niːʒn]
Pomona [pə'məʊnə]
Rancho de Aqua Caliente ['ræntʃəʊ daɪ 'ʌguːə kʌlɪ'entaɪ]
Redondo Beach [rə'dɒndəʊ]
Sacramento [sækrə'mentəʊ]
San Andreas [sæn æn'dreɪəs]
San Bernardino [sæn bɜːnə'diːnəʊ]
San Diego [sæn dɪ'eɪgəʊ]
San Gabriel [sæn 'geɪbrɪəl]
San Jose [sæn həʊ'zeɪ]
San Luis Obispo [sæn luːɪs ə'bɪspəʊ]
San Pedro [sæn 'peɪdrəʊ]
Santa Anita [sæntə ə'niːtə]
Santa Barbara [sæntə 'bɑːbrə]
Santa Clara [sæntə 'kleərə]
Santa Cruz [sæntə 'kruːz]
Santa Monica [sæntə 'mɒnɪkə]
Seuol [səʊl]
Sierra Nevadas [sɪ'erə nə'vædəz]
Solvang ['səʊlvæŋ]
Squaw Valley [skwɔː]
Stockton ['stɒktn]
Sunnyvale ['sʌnɪveɪl]
Tahoe ['tɑːhəʊ]
Tarzana [tɑː'zænə]
Temecula [tə'mekjuːlə]
Wyoming [waɪ'əʊmɪŋ]
Yale [jeɪl]
Yorba Linda [jɔːbə 'lɪndə]
Yosemite [jəʊ'semɪtɪ]
Yuma ['juːmə]

Other names

Angelus Temple ['ændʒələs 'tempəl]
Atari [ə'tɑːrɪ]
Christ [kraɪst]
Eiffel Tower ['aɪfəl]
El Dorado [el də'rɑːdəʊ]
Esalen Institute ['esələn]
Griffith Park ['grɪfɪθ]
Half Dome ['hɑːf dəʊm]
Hotel del Coronado [del kɒrə'nɑːdəʊ]
Mattel [mə'tel]
McIntosh ['mækɪntɒʃ]
Miami Vice [maɪ'æmɪ 'vaɪs]
Nuestra Señora de los Ángeles de Porciúncula [nu'estra sen'jɒrə de lɒs 'ɑːnheləs de pɒrsɪ'uːnkʊlə]
Tarzan ['tɑːzən]
Trans-America Building [trænzə'merɪkə 'bɪldɪŋ]
Universal Studios [juːnɪ'vɜːsl 'stjuːdɪəʊz]
Wells Fargo ['welz 'fɑːgəʊ]
Wham-O ['wæməʊ]